Nothing Rhymes with **Purple**

A Collection of Short Poems by Amanda Felts

Illustrations by Amanda Garner

Archway Publishing books may be ordered through booksellers or by contacting:

Archway Publishing
1663 Liberty Drive
Bloomington, IN 47403
www.archwaypublishing.com
844-669-3957

Because of the dynamic nature of the Internet, any web addresses or links contained in this book may have changed since publication and may no longer be valid. The views expressed in this work are solely those of the author and do not necessarily reflect the views of the publisher, and the publisher hereby disclaims any responsibility for them.

Interior Image Credit: Amanda Garner

ISBN: 978-1-6657-4153-8 (sc)
ISBN: 978-1-6657-4152-1 (hc)
ISBN: 978-1-6657-4151-4 (e)

Library of Congress Control Number: 2023905741

Print information available on the last page.

Archway Publishing rev. date: 05/24/2023

This book is dedicated to my parents,
for encouraging every rhyme.

One Man Band

Robbie plays the banjo,
He loves to play the sax.
The way he plays harmonica
Will stop you in your tracks.

He travels with his tuba
And his trusty tambourine.
He plays the ukulele
Like this world has never seen.

I've heard him on the xylophone,
A one man band indeed.
But when you listen to him
There is something you will need.

Buy yourself some earplugs,
The strongest pair they sell.
He plays all seven instruments,
But he doesn't play them well!

Vulture Pizza Parlor

I called the pizza parlor,
I was desperate for a pie.
The pizza parlor person
Named some toppings I should try.
"There's putrid pepperoni,
Rotten roadkill of the day,
Sour sausage, foul mushrooms,"
And I then I heard her say,
"I think you'll be quite happy with
Our rancid meat selection.
Our rats are kept in sunlight
So they're spoiled to perfection.
Our ingredients are never fresh,
And that's our guarantee.
If it doesn't taste like garbage,
Then your next one will be free!"
I just sat in silence
With their menu in my hand.
Vulture Pizza Parlor?
Oh, *now* I understand.

Stomach Seeds

Once I dared my buddy Jack
To eat a hundred seeds,
And now he needs a mower
Cuz his stomach's full of weeds.

The World is Full of Buts

The world is full of buts, my friend.
They're everywhere it seems.
Big buts, small buts, short and tall buts,
Tryin' to steal your dreams.

"But what if I can't do it?
What will happen if I fail?"
Those buts will often bother you
But don't let them prevail.

Take those doubts and hows and buts,
Your what ifs and your fears,
And gather up your "Yes I cans"
To kick them in their rears.

Although it's true, you'll sometimes fail
Just know, no matter what,
You'll never make your dreams come true
By sitting on your "buts."

Nothing Rhymes with Purple

If you've ever been a poet
Then you know it to be true,
When you try to rhyme with purple,
There is nothing you can do.

I love the color purple
And if it were up to me,
I would send a scuba diver
To the bottom of the sea.

He'd find a fish we've never found
Then give that fish a name.
With *squirples* in the world
Our lives would never be the same!

chirple
chirple!

I'd bet that in the tropics
I could find an unnamed bird.
A *yellow breasted churple*
That's a purple rhyming word!

8

Perhaps I'll cross two vegetables
And plant new hybrid seeds.
Come spring time I'd have *durples*
Growing in between the weeds.

It would mean the world to me
To write about a squirple,
And be the only human being
To rhyme a word with purple.

What is that you're saying?
My dream has taken flight?
I just rhymed with purple...
Hey, I guess you're right!

Horse Racin'

Don't bet against old Celery Sticks
When you go to the races.
He may sound like the slowest horse
And get a few last places,

But every now and then this horse
Will run so slow, he *wins*...
His race, he finally finishes
Just as the next begins.

It Get I Now

Start the at back be you'll why,
Finish finally you time the by
Smart you're if it read to try
Poem backwards a wrote I

Dear Reader,
This is a special sort of poem,
It must be read out loud.
Just follow the directions,
And I'm sure you'll make me proud!

The Fun Poem

Start reading with a whisper.
KEEP READING WITH A SHOUT!
Read this line with a giant grin,
And this one with a pout.
Read this part while you're marching
Like a soldier by your bed.
And this one while you're balancing
A pillow on your head.
Keep reading while you jog in place,
Then all the sudden FREEZE!
Start reading in slow motion
While your hands are on your knees.
Keep reading while you're jumping,
Keep reading while you dance.
Read this part while you run around
Like ants are in your pants.
Keep reading with a silly voice,
And when this poem is through.
Go ask your friends and family
To read it back to you!

Germ Collection

Rock collections, clock collections,
Baseball cards and bugs.
I suspect most kids collect
Old coins or dolls or mugs.

I've got a pal and this odd gal
Has jars of dirt and worms,
And used tissues and ear wax,
Cuz she loves collecting germs.

In the mood for rotten food?
She's got a toy box filled.
It's seeping but she's keeping all
The spoiled milk she's spilled.

And then, oh boy, her pride and joy
The chest of rancid meat.
She showed it to me last month
And for days I couldn't eat.

She may just break a record
With her ball of chewed-up gum.
She thinks landfills are gold mines
And that using soap is dumb.

I'm the only friend who'll bend
And play or talk or study
With this poor gal cuz no one wants
A germ collecting buddy.

Dirt Dessert

If an earthworm made you dinner
Do you think she would be hurt,
If she asked you how it tasted
And you said, "It tastes like dirt."

Sweet Tooth

"What's your favorite vegetable?",
I heard my dentist ask.
"There are so many good ones, sir,
That's such a daunting task!"

Then as he filled my cavity,
The seventh one he'd seen,
I told him with a silver smile,
"I think it's jelly beans!"

FRESH
JELLY
BEANS!!

18

I Thought I'd Rent a Rooster

I thought I'd rent a rooster,
I found one at the farm.
I kept him in my bedroom
To use as my alarm.

He's gone through all the cupboards.
I've got feathers in my bed.
My room is a disaster,
And he's got me seeing red.

He flew out of my window
Now he's tearing up the lawn.
All he cock-a-doodle-DOESN'T-do
Is wake me up at dawn!

A Penguin's Perspective

While walking through the zoo one day,
I heard a penguin crying.
I asked him what was wrong, he said,
"I'm just no good at flying.

The other birds can hit the skies
And soar up through the clouds,
But penguins never get to fly,
I guess we're not allowed."

I told him I would try to help,
"Don't get too down on things.
Just do what all the others do,
Just try to flap your wings."

His wings, they started flapping
But he didn't leave the ground.
We tried it with a steady breeze,
From a fan we found around.

That didn't work, so I advised
To try a running start.
He ran face first into a wall,
(I guess that wasn't smart.)

I said, "This is a last resort,
Leap off from over there."
I had him run off of a ledge
To start off in the air.

He took a leap and then he fell
And with a splash he hit.
And then he swam a figure-eight
While in his water pit.

He swam to shore and looked at me
With disappointed eyes.
"I guess that I'm a failure,
And I've used up all my tries."

"You're nuts!" I said, "I've never seen
A bird that *swims* like you.
Maybe you can't fly so well,
But you're good at what you do!"

"I guess I never thought of that,"
This penguin said to me.
"I may not see the *skies* like them,
But I get to see the *sea*."

22

Porcupine Embrace

I ran into a porcupine
Who said that he was feeling fine,
But when I went to say good-bye
My pokey pal began to cry.
I asked, "Is something bugging you?"
He said, "I felt like hugging you.
But hugs are something folks decline,
Who wants to hug a porcupine?"
"I see," I said, "I'll be right back."
I took my jacket off the rack
Along with mittens I'd been loaned
And every sweater that I owned.
I suited up and after that,
Taped on my plastic welcome mat.
Then with the suit that I'd designed
I hugged that poor old porcupine.
"Now I know," he laughed through tears,
"What I been missin' all these years!"

Blushing Maple

I heard a tree fart near my tree fort
While I lay in bed.
The tree was so embarrassed
That his green leaves turned to red.

24

Treehouse Intuition

I thought I'd build a treehouse
That would reach up to the sky,
But I didn't have a ladder
And I can't climb very high.

With a little intuition
And some sunlight, soon it seems,
My creation just may grow into
The treehouse of my dreams.

Secret Stew Recipe

Aunt Weatherbee, I have to say
This stew is quite divine!
Please let me see the recipe,
So I can make it mine.

"I'll show you what I've added
If you promise not to tell."
Her eyes got sharp and focused
Like a witch casting a spell.

"Ear wax mixed with deer tracks,
Some dandruff from a bear,
Two tablespoons of applesauce,
Three pairs of underwear...

A half a pound of lima beans
Some gopher guts and moss,
A quarter cup of curdled milk
Mixed with some gravy sauce.

And don't forget," she said to me,
"To add a dinner roll,
And stir in lots of water
Scooped out from your toilet bowl."

I shoved my plate aside and said,
"Well that explains its kick.
And if you'll please excuse me now,
I think I may be sick."

My Brilliant Idea

I'm certain I have a *fantastic* idea,
It's brilliant and one of a kind!
I bet if you looked high and low in this land
That no greater a thought you would find.

It's artistic and mystical, clever and wise,
A world-changing notion I'd bet.
Why haven't I shared this amazing idea?
Well, I just haven't thought of it yet.

Tire Swing

This tire swing is a wonderful thing,
My best idea so far.
I just hope Dad won't be too mad
When he tries to drive the car!

The Hair Fairy

Things have changed in Fairy Land,
I guess they got my letter.
I wrote them quite the note, you see,
On making aging better.

I'd lost a tooth and then at night
I'd placed it on my bed,
With hopes that I would wake to find
Some money there instead.

Of course, I love the Tooth Fairy,
But thought it quite unfair
That no one brings you money
When you age and lose your *hair*.

Cash for teeth, but *not* for hair?
What a shame indeed.
I wrote this in a letter
For the Tooth Fairy to read.

I think she must have paid the dues
With other fairies helping,
The next day I awoke to find
My balding father yelping!

He read the note that had been left,
His voice was light and merry.
"With every loss there is a gain,"
Signed, the new *Hair* Fairy.

So note this new addition to
The rules of how things work.
And when you're old, you'll thank me
For this new found, hair loss perk.

My Dog Ate My Homework

My dog, he ate my homework,
I promise that's the truth.
I bet there are some math problems
Still hanging from his tooth.

My sister is my witness,
She saw him eat it whole!
But please don't tell my teacher
That I put it in his bowl.

Snooze Button

A hibernating bear was sleeping soundly in his den.
His alarm clock starting buzzing at a quarter after ten,
"Rise and shine," his mother said, "It's time to catch some rays."
Instead he hit the snooze and slept another 30 days.

The Best Kind of Pet

Looking for a pet?
Get a rabbit if you're able.
Train it so at dinner time
It sneaks below the table,

And the salads, broccoli, carrots
That you didn't want to eat,
Will disappear like magic
Right before your very feet!

Giddy-Up

A horse brought me his laundry
And we stared at one another.
I guess he saw my ponytail
And thought I was his mother.

If It Started Raining Bubble Gum

If it started raining bubble gum,
I'd call my favorite fella.
"I hate to burst your bubble,
But please give back my gumbrella!"

Channel Changer

A goat ate my remote, and now
This pet that I've been raising
Is a stomach-churning, channel-turning
Mammal when he's grazing.

My Pet Invisi-Bull

Come meet this awesome creature that the pet store owner sold me!
He's one of only two world-wide, at least that's what he told me.
He called him an *invisi-bull*, and I was blown away.
Of course I had to buy him some *invisi-bails* of hay.
Invisi-bulls are special pets, so I thought, what the heck?
I'll buy him an *invisi-bell* to wear around his neck.
I couldn't keep from smiling, but I started feeling ill
When the pet store owner read to me my big *invisi-bill*.
What? Invisi-bulls aren't real? You think that he's a phony?
I can't believe I fell for that invisi-bull bologna!

Questions for a Walrus

I saw a walrus shopping
And I thought, is that a *mallrus?*
If he didn't tie his shoe lace,
Might he be a *trip and fallrus?*
Compared to other walruses
Is he a short or *tallrus?*
Suppose he was a *tallrus*
Was he good at *basketballrus?*
Does he have a baby brother?
Would his brother be a *crawlrus?*
It was then that I decided
I should go and ask the walrus,
But I turned and he was gone,
Like he was *never-there-at-allrus*.

Escalator Eddie and Elevator Eve

Escalator Eddie
And Elevator Eve
Have different ways of comin'
And different ways to leave.

An *up and down* relationship
Is what this couple shares.
All they can agree on
Is NOT to take the stairs.

The Firefly

A firefly flew right into
A spider web one night.
He didn't see it coming,
Guess he wasn't very bright.

Pryer is a Liar

The bold and daring Mr. Pryer,
Thought he'd walk across a wire.
Set it up, said, "Make it higher.
Watch, I'll cross it on a tire."
Saw the ground, said "Add some briar.
Still too easy, start a fire.
Find me a good blindfold tie-er.
I want music, bring the choir!"
Saw him starting to perspire
Left us little to admire
Though he is a fearless crier,
Mr. Pryer is a liar.

Growth Spurt

My sister Flo loved sourdough, she ate it every day.
One time she ate two bowls of it and then went out to play.
The summer sun was cookin' when she heard my mother call her.
The yeast in it had risen and she'd grown 6 inches taller.